Youth Master of Business Administration Series

Accounting

A learning workbook program for junior high and high school students.

Visit the Y.M.B.A. website at www.YMBAgroup.com

ISBN-13: 978-1725514416
ISBN-10: 1725514419
Printed by CreateSpace, An Amazon.com Company.
Available from Amazon.com and other retail outlets.
CreateSpace, Charleston, SC

Copyright protected © 2015, 2018, 2020
All rights reserved.
This workbook publication, or any part of this book, may not be reproduced, distributed, stored in a retrieval system, or transmitted in any form for any purpose without prior written approval from the autho

Consult a professional when seeking business advice and decisions. This is a learning book discussing topics in a general style, not intended to be considered professional advice, suggestions, or guidance.

Submit all inquiries at the website www.YMBAgroup.com

Y.M.B.A. Accounting - grades 6 7 8 9 10 +   ages 12 13 14 15 16 +

Accounting

We hope to hear from you!

We value your suggestions.

Positive feedback, shares and word of mouth appreciated.

Suggestions, Comments, Questions

always welcome at

www.YMBAgroup.com

THE Y.M.B.A. GROUP - ACCOUNTING
Accounting, Economics, and Budgeting

TABLE OF CONTENTS

How To Use This Learning Workbook	7
What Is Accounting	8
Assets Are Valuable (LIFO, FIFO)	10
Liabilities Cost Money (A/P, A/R)	16
The Balance Sheet	20
Sales Create Revenue	24
Business Expenses	26
The Income Statement	32
Business Ratios	36
Supply and Demand	42
The Marketplace Sets A Price	46
A Better Budget	48
Macroeconomics - The Big Picture	52
Microeconomics	54
Case Study	56
Accounting Review Quiz	59
Answer Key	67
Completion Certificate	72

Do you have a suggestion for a book topic?

Let us know and we may create it!

www.YMBAgroup.com

How To Use This Book

Thank you for choosing the Y.M.B.A. learning workbook series. I am excited to share the topics with you. As a teacher, corporate professional, M.B.A. and parent, I sought to find a quality program for my children that was both at an introductory level and interesting for their age. When I discovered nothing like this existed, Y.M.B.A. began. A business learning program for young students created and designed by an M.B.A, teacher, and parent. Y.M.B.A. presents information in clear, easy to follow style; focused on students approximately 12 to 16 years of age. I designed the lessons as a combination textbook and workbook because students retain far more when applying the newly taught ideas. The series instructs one idea at a time in a clear and simple to understand format. While presenting students with a concept they develop their understanding with fun, level-appropriate, examples. After each lesson page is a worksheet to apply the idea from the page prior. This pattern keeps students engaged and actively learning by seeking on-going student applications. The "The Drawing Board" worksheets reinforce the lesson as students practice reasoning, computation, or analysis. The Y.M.B.A. focuses on useful business concepts and everyday topics found across industries and in daily life.

Each learning workbook has a quiz for a student demonstration of their new understanding of the subject. As the student completes the learning workbook you will likely see an increase in both pride and confidence. Why wait for business concepts to be introduced? Students are ready to learn about practical life and business topics today. Y.M.B.A. lessons include relevant examples based on familiar student scenarios to sustain learning that is both effective and fun!

Business skills are utilized in every industry; an understanding of business is essential. Why wait? Students can begin achieving more with Y.M.B.A. today and build a path for the future. Your support is appreciated. Suggestions, questions, or comments are always welcome.

Thank you,

L.J. Keller

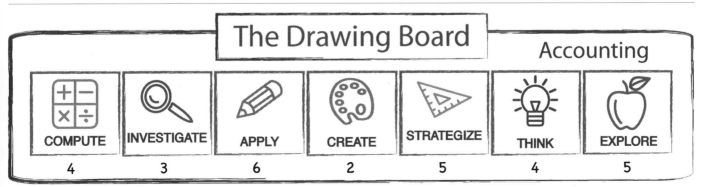

The quantity of each skill practice area is shown below each learning tile. Worksheet pages seek to capture student interest and build learning momentum.

What Is Accounting?

Accounting keeps a record of the activities of a business. These records provide owners and managers with data when making decisions. Data can show patterns to help business managers choose future decisions.

Luckily there is a set of rules for how to record business transactions known as GAAP. This set of standard rules makes it possible for accounting statements to be easily understood regardless of who created the statements.

For example, consider RubbAir Tire Company. The company sold 145 tires last December and 141 tires December two years ago. Upon reviewing the accounting records, the inventory manager would plan to have at least 145 tires in stock for the upcoming December.

GAAP
Generally **A**ccepted **A**ccounting **P**rincipals
Instructions and rules accountants follow to keep reports standard and understandable.

Consolidated
Refers to gathered results of business operations that are shown on the accounting statements. Operations is the buying and selling at a company.

The information gathered and maintained by accountants is consolidated (brought together) in the financial statements for a company. Two common financial statements for a company are a balance sheet and an income statement.

Balance Sheet *shows* What The Company Owns *and* What The Company Owes

Income Statement *shows* What The Company Sells *and* What The Company Spends

Accounting Careers

Inventory Manager	Tax Accountant	Invoice Clerk
Chief Financial Officer	Budget Manager	Accounts Payable Clerk (A/P Clerk)
Bookkeeper	Payroll Processor	Certified Public Accountant (CPA)

The Drawing Board

Data Decisions

Imagine you are the inventory control manager at RubbAir Tire Company. Review the accounting data below and calculate the result.

1. The company spent $3,045 on tires in December to purchase a total of 145 tires. How much did one tire cost the company?
   The cost per tire was: $ _____

2. The company sold 145 tires to customers in December. The sale price per tire was $85 each. What is the total sales revenue (how much customers paid)?
   The total sales revenue was: $ _____

3. The state requires the company to charge 7% sales tax to customers on their purchases. How much sales tax was collected with the sale of 145 tires?
   The total state sales tax collected was: $ _____

4. The profit the company earned by selling 145 tires is equal to the total tire sales less the cost of purchasing the tires from the tire supplier.
   What is the profit for these tires?
   The profit from selling the 145 tires is: $ _____

5. A supplier has just informed the company that the price of tires has increased to $25 per tire. How much will the company spend to purchase the same number of tires next year?
   The cost of purchasing 145 tires next year will be: $ _____

COMPUTE

Assets Are Valuable

Asset
Anything that has monetary value and is owned.

Did you know that you have assets! Anything that is owned and can be sold for any amount of money is an asset. Perhaps a toy? A book? A movie?

Monetary Value
An item having the ability to be sold for cash.

When a business begins, one of the first activities is to gather *things*. These *things* may be equipment, office supplies, uniforms, furniture, business cards, marketing signs, computers, or inventory. Each of these purchases made by the company are recorded in the company accounting journals as a decrease in the cash asset account and an increase in another account.

TANGIBLE ASSET any object that has value and is a physical item.

INTANGIBLE ASSET a non-physical item of value.

Tangible Assets
Cash
Inventory
Vehicles

Intangible Assets
Goodwill
Patents
Copyrights

Ledgers - The records of a company where buying and selling transactions are written, known as "the company books".

The Cash Asset

Cash is the most common asset for any company and perhaps the most wanted. However, a company must decrease the cash balance when spending money to buy other assets. For example, to have a product available to sell to a customer, a business will deduct money from the cash account to purchase inventory. The value of the inventory is the same as the price the company pays to buy the inventory.

The cash asset account will decrease by the amount spent.
The inventory asset account will increase the same amount.

The equal amount taken from one asset account (cash) and added to another asset account (inventory) results in no change to the total asset value of a company.

Copyright Protected.   www.YMBAgroup.com

The Drawing Board

Would You Rather

Circle the asset below that has a higher dollar value to the company.

1. (a) Checking account, value $3,000   (b) Savings account, value $4,000

2. (a) Office copier, value $900   (b) Office printer, value $400

3. (a) Office supplies, value $300   (b) Cleaning supplies, value $150

4. (a) Inventory, 10 cases at $120 each   (b) Inventory, 21 cases at $85 each

5. (a) 18 Stock shares at $4.35 each   (b) 32 Stock shares at $2.50 each

6. (a) 4 Trucks, value $9,200 each   (b) 6 Cars, value $7,800 each

7. (a) 12 Uniforms, value $42 each   (b) 35 Promotional t-shirts, value $8 each

8. (a) 4 Computers, value $930 each   (b) 7 Televisions, value $345 each

9. (a) 3,200 Labels, value .20¢   (b) 210 Shipping boxes, value $1.85 each

10. (a) 9 Desks, value $125 each   (b) 45 Chairs, value $95 each

CURRENT ASSET is cash, or can be sold for cash, within one year or less.

NON-CURRENT ASSET any item of value that will take one year or more to sell.

STRATEGIZE

Meet LIFO - Last In, First Out

A company buys inventory and then wants to sell the inventory as products to retail customers. Before a product is sold, the company lists the products as assets in the *inventory* account. Over time inventory may include similar items purchased by the company at different prices. Using the **Last In, First Out** inventory method, **the most recent price the company paid to buy the inventory is considered the value of the sold product**. The most recent price the company paid to buy the item is the amount the inventory account is reduced when the inventory is sold.

For example, imagine a retail customer purchases a jump rope from Sports Den for $3.00. Sports Den purchased jump ropes from the supplier this year for $1.75 each. Last year jump ropes were also bought from the same supplier, but for $1.20 each. The accounting records will use the value of $1.75 when computing how much to reduce the company inventory as a result of the retail sale. Sports Den using LIFO considers the higher-priced inventory as the amount to reduce the inventory account.

LIFO
The last *purchased* inventory is the first *sold* inventory.

Sports Den sold a total of 32 jump ropes in August. The jump ropes retail price is $3.00 each. Sports Den purchased jump ropes from the manufacturer this year for $1.75 each and last year for $1.20 each. Since Sports Den uses the LIFO method of inventory reduction the total inventory value will reduce by $56.00.

Total jump ropes sold x most recent jump rope purchase price if $1.75 each.

    32   x $1.75   = $56.00

Inventory Remaining: 20 jump ropes bought at $1.75 and 60 jump ropes bought at $1.20.

Sports Den Accounts August, 2020	
Jump Rope Inventory August 1, 2020	$11,400
Less Jump Ropes Sold In August, 2020	$56
Jump Rope Inventory August 31, 2020	$11,344

The Drawing Board

Reducing With LIFO

Consider the recent sales at Sports Den. Find the total dollar amount the inventory will be reduced using the LIFO method.

1. 16 volleyballs were sold in the month of September.

    Retail cost per volleyball: $14.00

    75 volleyball's purchased for inventory in August, 2020: $6.00

    Inventory cost per volleyball purchased August, 2019: $5.00

    Inventory reduction value using LIFO: $ _____

2. 52 pairs of Zip running sneakers were sold in August, 2020.

    Retail cost per pair of Zip running sneakers: $30.00

    85 sneakers purchased for inventory in May, 2019: $12.00

    Inventory cost per pair of sneakers purchased August, 2018: $9.00

    Inventory reduction value using LIFO: $ _____

3. 214 baseballs were sold in the month of August.

    Retail cost per baseball: $4.00

    300 baseball's purchased for inventory in September, 2020: $2.50

    Inventory cost per baseball purchased March, 2019: $2.00

    Inventory reduction value using LIFO: $ _____

4. 25 4-person tents were sold in August.

    Retail cost per 4-person tent: $89.00

    40 4-person tent's purchased for inventory in June, 2020: $50.00

    Inventory cost per 4-person tent purchased April, 2019 $47.00

    Inventory reduction value using LIFO: $ _____

COMPUTE

Meet FIFO - First In, First Out

Food-Mart uses the FIFO method when accounting for the inventory. When the grocery store purchases food, the items are presented on the shelves for customers. As the inventory clerk organizes the food new purchases are placed behind the older purchases on a shelf to make sure the closer expiration dates are purchased first. Since most foods have expiration dates, Food-Mart uses FIFO when placing a dollar value on their store inventory.

July Inventory: 60
December 1st Sold 20

July inventory: 44
December 1st sold: 44

Food-Mart purchased the milk with expiration dates of November 21, 2020 from Cow Country for $1.00 each. Food-Mart also bought milk with the expiration date December 12, 2020 from Mooosic Cow for $1.24 each.

FIFO
The first *purchased* inventory is the first *sold* inventory.

Food-Mart does not change the retail price of the milk. Each week shoppers are offered either brank for $2.15 each. Food-Mart sold a total of 64 cartons of milk December 1. Since they use FIFO inventory is computed as selling all 44 with the November 21, 2020 date and 20 with the expiration of December 12, 2020

What is the sales adjustment made to the milk inventory when using the FIFO method?

Step 1: Find the inventory value of the November expiration date milk that sold:

Food-Mart purchase price: $1.00   Quantity sold to customers: 44

$_____

Step 2: Find the inventory value of the sold December expiration date milk:

Food-Mart purchase price: $1.24   Quantity sold to customers: 20

$_____

Step 3: What is the dollar amount the inventory value will be reduced due to sales on December 1? (add the results, step 1 + step 2) $_____

APPLY

The Drawing Board

Accounting Terms

Match the term with the word it is describing.
Draw a line to match the term to the definition.

- current asset
- LIFO
- liability
- FIFO
- account
- non-current asset
- tangible asset
- inventory
- intangible asset

- An amount a company owes, a debt to pay.
- The inventory method that values sold inventory based on the first purchased cost.
- An item owned by a company that is cash or can be sold for cash in one year or less.
- A place to group similar revenues, expenses, assets, or liabilities in accounting.
- The inventory method that values sold inventory based on the last purchased cost.
- An item owned by a company that is cash or can be sold for cash in more than one year.
- A non-physical item that adds value to the activity of a business.
- Goods held by a company that are offered for sale to customers.
- A physical item that has a money value.

EXPLORE

Liabilities Cost Money

What is a liability?
A liability is a balance owed. When a good or service is exchanged the buyer and seller complete a transaction. The transaction to pay for the item may not be completed at the same time the good is traded, or the service is completed.

Short-Term Liabilities - (due in less than one year)
When a company purchases an item the seller may agree to receive payment at a later date. The seller will send an invoice to the customer. The invoice will include the balance due and payment terms. Payment terms detail when the seller expects payment to be completed. The payment terms may also include a late fee if payment is after the due date.

Common Invoice Terms
Due On Receipt - Full payment is due when the invoice is received.
Net 10 - Full payment is due 10 days or less from the invoice date.
Net 15 - Full payment is due 15 days or less from the invoice date.
Net 30 - Full payment is due 30 days or less from the invoice date.

Long-Term Liabilities - (due in greater than one year)
Expenses are not always due in the short term. A company may have a loan that is due over a range of months, or even years. Examples of these long-term liabilities include car loans and mortgages. Generally, car loans and mortgages are both large dollar amounts, so the lender agrees to accept a partial payment each month until the full balance is paid. Car loans and mortgages have interest charges added to the amount owed. Interest is the extra money charged by the company that made the loan. The loan amount, plus the interest charges are paid to $0 to be considered paid in full.

The Drawing Board

What To Pay?

Three invoices for ColorTube Printers Corp. are shown below. The stamp on each shows the date the invoice was paid. Enter the amount that should have been paid based on the date the invoice was paid in the area provided.

Examine each invoice for the terms and late fees, if any, to add to the balance due.

National Paper Supply House, Inc.

INVOICE NUMBER: 8752   December 7, 2020

DUE DATE: DECEMBER 21, 2020, NET 15

Quantity	Stock Number	Item Details	Each	Total Price
12	472G			$180.00
10	657R		$9	$99.00

PAID DECEMBER 28, 2020

Sub-Total $279.00
State Sales Tax 7% $19.53
Total $298.53

IF PAID BEYOND NET 10 ADD $25 LATE FEE.

1. Payment Amount

$ _____

Better Brown Box Business Company

INVOICE NUMBER: 1074   December 12, 2020

DUE DATE: NET 30 FROM INVOICE DATE

2. Payment Amount

$ _____

Quantity	Stock Number	Item Details		Total Price
100	FB4	Standard		$470.00
100	FQ5			$310.00

PAID DECEMBER 28, 2020

Sub-Total $780.00
State Sales Tax 6% $46.80
Total $826.80

Rush Flash Delivery Service   **Monthly Statement**

INVOICE NUMBER: D435   December 18, 2020

DUE DATE: DUE ON RECEIPT OF INVOICE. AFTER 10 DAYS ADD A 10% LATE FEE.

3. Payment Amount

$ _____

Quantity	Stock Number	Item Details	Total Price
24	32h7	Same day	$96.00
18	58m9		$360.00

PAID DECEMBER 30, 2020

Sub-Total $456.00
State Sales Tax 8% $36.48
Total $492.48

APPLY

Accounts Receivable and Payable

**Accounts Receivable
The account for money owed to the company.**

The Accounts Receivable account is an asset account for the company that includes the balances owed to the company from customers. The balances due are generally expected to be paid in full in one year or less. Amounts not paid within the timeframe selected by the company (printed on the invoice) are considered past due. Past due accounts may be shared with another business known as a *collections company*. The service offered by a collections company is that they will contact the debtor (who owes the money) and arrange for payment to be completed. Late payments are often reported on an personal, or a company, credit report. For this reason businesses (and people) often seek to pay balances due by the company printed on the invoice. When a customer does not pay their invoice, and collections have not been successful, a business will move the amount due from the accounts payable account to the allowance for doubtful accounts. Since it is doubtful (unlikely) the customer will pay the balance it is no longer included in the company asset account. If a customer never pays the balance it is recorded as a business expense.

**Accounts Payable
The account for money the company has to pay.**

The Accounts Payable journal account is a liability account for the company. You may recall a liability is an amount owed by the company. When a company makes a purchase and does not complete payment at the same time a liability is created. The purchase is recorded in the company records as an increase to the asset account since a new asset was purchased. There is also a second entry to increase the liability account (accounts payable) since the company still has to pay for the purchase. The company will receive an invoice with the balance due. The invoice will include details about the balance owed payment due date.

Accounts Payable are generally due in one year or less. Amounts due in more than one year will likely use the account *Long Term Debt* or *Loans Payable*.

The Drawing Board

Pay or Receive?

In each of the boxes below is a transaction involving Royal Films Movie Theater. Draw a line from each box to either the accounts payable oval, or the accounts receivable oval, to indicate if the transaction is a receivable or a payable for the movie theater. Remember, if the company purchased the item and owes the money, the amount due will be shown in the *accounts payable* account. If the movie theater sold the item and is waiting to receive payment, the amount is recorded in the *accounts receivable* account.

ACCOUNTS PAYABLE

Invoices The Company Pays

Money Paid To Suppliers

- Movie Theater Advertising Local Town Billboards
- Movie Poster Lobby Display Picture Frame Replacements
- Monthly Electric Company Utility Invoice
- Party Room Rental Contract Payment Due
- Private Movie Screening Contract Payment Due
- Movie Preview Audience Advertising Commercials

Money Paid By Customers

Amounts The Company Collects

ACCOUNTS RECEIVABLE

EXPLORE

The Balance Sheet

A simple formula is used to compute business results on the Balance Sheet.

Total Assets are equal to Total Liabilities plus Owners Equity

The balance sheet shows how much a company would be worth if all the company bills were paid. The worth of a company (equity) is equal to the amount of the assets, minus what the company owes and the amount owned by owners.

Riddle: When does one equal two?

Answer: When keeping track of where assets move in a company.

Each spending or buying action by a company causes two results.

One Account Decreases  One Account Increases

In accounting each part of the transaction is entered into a specific account. The account will keep a record of the updated account balance. A company with up to date account balances will have accurate information to review when making decisions.

Consider this example at Thirty Fields Sports Company who just purchased a new golf cart. The golf cart will be used by the maintenance team as they move from field to field completing service requests. The company wrote a check for $7,000 to purchase the golf cart. The check will decrease the cash account by $7,000. The company now owns the golf cart. This will increase the value of the company equipment by $7,000. Since the company is moving the value of $7,000 from one account (cash) to another account (equipment) the total assets of the company do not change. The amount the cash decreases is the same amount the equipment increases.

Total Assets Before Golf Cart Purchase: $62,450.00

Cash Account		Equipment Account	
Current Balance:	$24,270.00	Current Balance:	$19,350.00
Less Payment Made:	$7,000.00	Plus Purchase Made:	$7,000.00
Ending Balance Cash:	$17,270.00	Ending Balance Equipment:	$26,350.00

Total Assets After Golf Cart Purchase: $62,450.00

The Drawing Board

Balance Me

Your job today is to be an accounting superhero. Fill in the missing number to help each company complete their balance sheet. For each of the open spaces enter the amount needed to balance the accounts.

ASSETS = LIABILITIES + OWNERS EQUITY

1. Balance Sheet
1/1/2019 - 12/31/2019

Assets:
Cash	10,000
Accounts Receivable	500
Inventory	3,000
Vehicles	6,000

Liabilities:
Accounts Payable	1,000
Mortgage Payable	2,500
Car Loan:	____

Owners Equity: 7,000

2. Balance Sheet
1/1/2019 - 12/31/2019

Assets:
Cash	21,000
Checking Account	4,800
Savings Account	4,200
Accounts Receivable:	7,300
Computers	4,200
Inventory	6,000
Equipment	3,500
Vehicles	9,000

Liabilities:
Accounts Payable	1,000
Mortgage Payable	5,800
Car Loan	3,000

Owners Equity: ____

3. Balance Sheet
1/1/2019 - 12/31/2019

Assets:
Cash	____
Checking Account	11,800
Savings Account	7,200
Accounts Receivable	7,300
Computers	4,400
Inventory	8,000
Equipment	3,500
Vehicles	2,000

Liabilities:
Accounts Payable	1,000
Mortgage Payable	5,800
Car Loan	3,000

Owners Equity: 28,000

4. Balance Sheet
1/1/2019 - 12/31/2019

Assets:
Cash	12,000
Accounts Receivable	800
Inventory:	3,200
Vehicles	7,000

Liabilities:
Accounts Payable	2,400
Mortgage Payable	3,200
Car Loan	5,000

Owners Equity: ____

STRATEGIZE

Balance Sheet Terms

Liabilities + Owners Equity equal Assets

Define "Current"
A CURRENT ASSET can be converted into cash in one year or less.

A CURRENT LIABILITY is expected to be paid in one year or less.

Define "Pre-Paid"
A pre-paid expense is paid by a company before the company uses the purchase. Most common with electric, telephone, rent, insurance and taxes. For example, the insurance bill is paid every three months for the next three months of coverage. After the bill is paid, and until the paid dates arrive, the invoice is pre-paid.

Define "Doubtful Accounts"
Doubtful accounts are customer accounts of a business that are past the due date for payment and the customer is not responding to payment requests.

Define "Fixed Asset"
A fixed asset generally has a high dollar value and would take about 1 year or longer to be available as cash to the owner.

Define "Stockholders Equity" and "Owners Equity"
The amount the owners have invested directly into the company and the amount they are owed from the assets of a company.

Did you ever wonder ... How can a mortgage be both a current liability and a long term liability?
Answer: A mortgage is a loan where the lender provides the money so the company may purchase a building. In return, the company will owe the amount borrowed, plus an added amount, interest. A payment is due each month to pay part of the balance due. Mortgages may take as long as 30 years to be paid. After the borrowed amount, and the interest, is paid to the lender, the loan will be paid in full.

Copyright Protected.   www.YMBAgroup.com

The Drawing Board

Build and Balance

Complete the balance sheet by entering an amount next to each account using the clues provided at the bottom of the page. After all clues are in place use addition and subtraction to enter the amounts for the remaining accounts.

Assets = Liabilities + Equity

Splashy Swimming Pools
Balance Sheet
January 1, 2019 – December 31, 2019

Assets

Current Assets

Cash	$33,000	
Accounts Receivable	$2,000	(1)
(less doubtful accounts)	($200)	(2)
Inventory	$6,000	(3)
Prepaid Expenses	$800	
Total Current Assets	$41,600	(4)

Fixed Assets

Land	$30,600	(5)
Building	$75,000	(6)
Equipment	$21,000	(7)
Furniture	$4,000	
Total Fixed Assets	$130,600	(8)

Total Assets	$172,200	(9)

Liabilities

Current Liabilities

Accounts Payable	$7,200	
Loan Payments Due	$2,800	(10)
Taxes Payable	$4,000	(11)
Total Current Liabilities	$14,000	

Long-Term Liabilities

Mortgage	$45,000	
Equipment Loan	$15,800	
Total Long Term Liabilities	$60,800	(12)

Total Liabilities	$74,800	(13)
Owners Equity	$97,800	
Liabilities + Equity	$172,600	

---

1. Splashy Swimming Pools is owed $2,000 from customers, but have listed $200 of the amount as not likely to be paid.
2. Splashy purchased $800 in inventory to be added to the existing inventory balance of $5,200.
3. Total assets for Splashy are $182,000 including the building for $75,000 and the land it is on for $30,600.
4. Equipment has the same value as last year, $21,000.
5. The company just received a $4,000 tax bill.

THINK

Sales Create Revenue

A sale happens when a good or service is traded among buyers and sellers. A company goal is to have an increasing sales amount to earn an increasing profit.

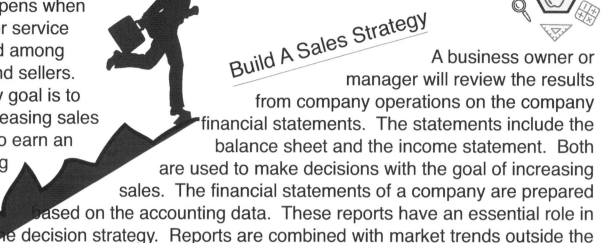

Build A Sales Strategy

A business owner or manager will review the results from company operations on the company financial statements. The statements include the balance sheet and the income statement. Both are used to make decisions with the goal of increasing sales. The financial statements of a company are prepared based on the accounting data. These reports have an essential role in the decision strategy. Reports are combined with market trends outside the company to plan the overall strategy on how to increase sales each quarter.

Financial statements are most helpful when an owner or manager can examine the current accounting period results along with the prior timeframes. An accounting period can be either a month, a quarter, or a year of business operations. By looking at the historical patterns and trends a company can identify aspects to help make better decisions to achieve company goals.

REVENUE MINUS EXPENSES = PROFIT

Time In The Accounting Department

A full accounting cycle refers to one year (12 months) of business operations. Most businesses in the United States use a **FISCAL YEAR** that follows the common calendar. A business that considers a new accounting cycle to begin each year on the 1st of January is said to follow a calendar-year fiscal schedule. To compare shorter timeframes of business operations accounting records are divided into quarters. A fiscal year schedule divides the year into quarters as:

January 1 to March 31 is the 1st quarter.

April 1 to June 30 is the 2nd quarter of the year.

July 1 to September 30 is the 3rd quarter of the year.

October 1 to December 31 is the 4th quarter of the year.

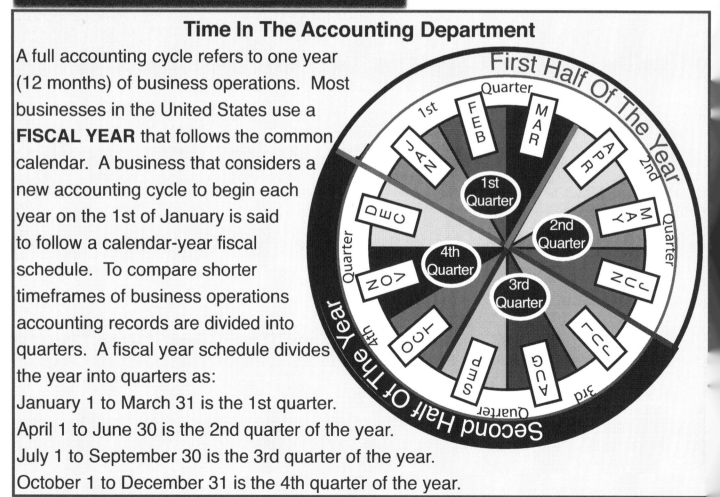

The Drawing Board

Time To Time

Choosing the most useful combination of financial statements to examine will help make an effective decision. For the questions below select the more helpful group of financial statements.

1. The company is planning on purchasing inventory for the Thanksgiving Holiday Bonanza. The manager should review:
   (a) the last 24 years of statements   (b) the last 3 years of statements

2. The company is considering payroll increases and would like to know how much the payroll has increased since the company opened in 2007.
   (a) all Balance Sheets available   (b) last years Balance Sheet

3. Two years ago the company bought a new fuel-efficient car to help reduce the fuel expense for the business. The manager would like to see if there has been a savings in fuel costs.
   (a) the last 8 months of statements   (b) the last 4 years of statements.

4. The company received the annual tax bill and would like to compare it to last years tax expense.
   (a) last years Balance Sheet   (b) last quarters Balance Sheet

5. The owner believes the new furniture bought last month was $1,000. Where can the owner see the sales results from last month?
   (a) last months Balance Sheet   (b) last years Balance Sheet

6. The accountant has requested the total assets for each of the past 5 years. Which financial reports would be the most helpful?
   (a) 5 years of Balance Sheets   (b) 5 quarters of Balance Sheets

BONUS:
   7. What month is the first month in the first quarter of a fiscal year?
   _____

   8. What are the months in the 2nd quarter?
   _____

INVESTIGATE

Business Expenses

Starting a business is a risk. There is no guarantee that a business will be successful - even with the best product or invention. When someone has an idea for a company, they will invest their time and money to start the business. The investment is made with the hope that the concept will create a product or service customers will purchase. When a business is not successful, the owner has lost the money they invested. The chance of success is the motivation to start a company.

◆ ◆ ◆

Establishing a business costs money. The company will need to be registered and insured. Once established standard expense accounts, such as office supplies, computers, uniforms, and telephone, will begin to be bought, so there will be accounting records to show the owner's investment in the business.

◆ ◆ ◆

One of the more costly investments when starting a company is marketing. Marketing will let potential customers know about the product, the product price, where it may be purchased, and of any promotions being offered by the company.
This is known as *the Four P's of Marketing*.

The Balancing Act

Finding the balance between spending enough money on marketing and being able to pay expenses is done by monitoring financial reports in a business. By knowing which marketing promotions resulted in customers making a purchase is an essential aspect of a successful company. The daily expenses, also known as **fixed expenses, need to be paid each month even if there are $0 in sales**. For example, the business rent is due to be paid every month - even if zero items have sold. The owners will plan to balance the available money to make sure the company can pay the fixed expenses.

Product	Price
4 P's of Marketing	
Place	Promotion

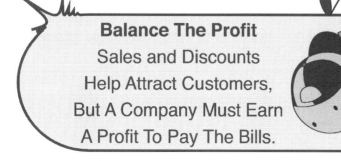

Balance The Profit
Sales and Discounts
Help Attract Customers,
But A Company Must Earn
A Profit To Pay The Bills.

Balance The Expenses
To Be Sure The
Company Can Pay
The Bills - Even With
Zero Dollars In Sales.

The Drawing Board

Make A Plan

Hooray! You just received your file confirmation in the mail from the Secretary of State for your state. Your corporation is officially registered!

1. Circle your new company industry from the choices in toolbox one below.

TOOLBOX ONE

> Dentist Bakery Ski Instructor Lawn Service
>
> Photographer Dog Walker Book Store Shoe Store

2. Next, consider the purchases your company will buy to meet the needs of your customers. Circle four expense accounts that your company will use to record the transactions for those purchases.

TOOLBOX TWO

> Utilities Office Supplies Inventory Rent or Mortgage
>
> Insurance Uniforms Equipment Educational Training

3. List the four expense categories circled in Toolbox 2. Next, list two possible purchases that may be recorded within each account.

Expense 1: _____   Expense 2: _____

purchase: _____   purchase: _____

purchase: _____   purchase: _____

Expense 3: _____   Expense 4: _____

purchase: _____   purchase: _____

purchase: _____   purchase: _____

CREATE

Long-Term Expenses

Long term expenses are company spending that is paid back to the lender one payment at a time. Paying back a debt (balance due) by making several payments until the amount due is paid in full is known as an installment payment plan. Generally, an installment payment plan includes an additional charge, known as interest, that is also due to be paid to the lender.

Examples of long term expenses for a business include mortgages, car loans, or large equipment or machinery loans. Each of these different expense types have their own category in the company accounts. When a payment is made, or a new purchase is completed, the transaction will be recorded by accounting in a specific account.

Fill in the blanks for your letter below - the first day of your new job as President!

My friend,

Today I was promoted to become the youngest president in the history of the _____ Company. At the company I was excited to make my first few
(your favorite color)

purchases as President _____. For my new office, I purchased a
(your first name)

_____ and a _____ at a cost of $75 and was able to use the company
(an office supply)   (an office supply)

credit card. For the shipping area, I made arrangements for a bank loan to purchase the HMJ-17 packing machine. The bank loan amount is $6,875. My assistant, known as _____ the _____, received an email from the warehouse
(friends name)   (an animal)

manager requesting three hand trucks at the cost of $80 each. I approved the request to buy the hand trucks and Hand-Trucks USA will be mailing an invoice.

I am excited to review the accounting statements to see the many ways I will help bring the company into the future!

Visit with you soon,

Company President

CREATE

The Drawing Board

Work The Plan

Attention: Bookkeeper, Accounts Payable Clerk, and Budget Manager
Date: June 12, 2020
From: Operations Manager
Re: Company increasing service area to three new zip codes

Have a BoInG Day.

As discussed at our meeting, the owners of BoInG Bounce Houses have voted to approve a customer service area expansion. The company will seek customers in three new zip codes. This will bring the service area to a total of four zip codes.

The population and income of the three new zip codes are the same as the current zip code. There is a minimal amount of competition. For these reasons, the marketing team has stated they expect the same amount of customer demand. To stay a top company, we will offer the super-bounce mega-water features. Remember to include the Bouncin' Bubbles in the price history.

We ask your departments for a summary of the bounce house purchases over the last three years. This will allow the owners to make reliable decisions about how many new bounce houses to purchase. Also, a second report is requested. The owners need to hire employees to set up and take down the bounce house rentals. How many hours the four employees currently perform bounce house installs and returns each month?

The information is requested by email before June 26, 2020.

Read the internal office memo above. An internal memo is sent inside a company. A memo may be sent by email, or printed on a piece of paper. Answer the following:

1. Why do you think the company needs to buy bounce houses?

2. How can the current inventory number help the owners plan the purchase?

3. What would be the math formula to help the owners compute the number of employees to hire for the new zip code installs and returns?

_____ X _____ = _____

THINK

Short-Term Expenses

Short-term expenses are the amount the company owes that has to be paid back in less than one year. The majority of short-term expenses are due in 30 days or less. Examples include electric, telephone, and credit card bills. Each of these expenses will be entered into an expense category for the business.

The Bull Pen, a sports company, buys two dozen file folders and asks Speedy Supplies to mail an invoice.

Office Supplies account increases $22 to include the new asset.

Accounts Payable increases $22 to include for the added debt.

The Authors Pen, a book company, buys a new binding printer and gives a $6,435 check payment to Speedy Supplies.

Machinery account increases $6,435 to include the added asset.

Checking decreases $6,435 since money was spent from the checking account.

The Dog Pen, a dog training business, buys a puppy grooming service kit and arranges for a bank loan of $8,340.

Equipment account increases $8,340 to include the added asset.

Bank Loan increases $8,340 to include the money now owed to the bank for the loan.

Sample Chart of Accounts

Account Name	Type	Account Name	Type
Checking	Asset	Accounts Payable	Liability
Accounts Receivable	Asset	Credit Card	Liability
Office Supplies	Asset	Bank Loan	Liability
Machinery	Asset	Taxes Payable	Liability
Equipment	Asset	Retained Earnings	Owners Equity

The Drawing Board

Hoop-De-Doo

Examine the Chart of Accounts on the previous page to answer the questions below. First, in section (A), circle the two accounts affected by the transaction. On line (B), circle to select if the transaction will cause the checking account to "increase", "decrease", or if the transaction will create "no change".
Reminder, one account will increase, and one will decrease with each purchase.

1. Hula Trio Corp. uses a loan to buy a new hula-hoop bending machine.

(A) Account Name	Type	Account Name	Type
Checking	Asset	Accounts Payable	Liability
Accounts Receivable	Asset	Credit Card	Liability
Office Supplies	Asset	Bank Loan	Liability
Machinery	Asset	Taxes Payable	Liability
Equipment	Asset	Retained Earnings	Owners Equity

(B)   (a) increase   (b) decrease   (c) no change

2. The accountant at the Hula Trio Corp. pays $700 on a credit card.

(A) Account Name	Type	Account Name	Type
Checking	Asset	Accounts Payable	Liability
Accounts Receivable	Asset	Credit Card	Liability
Office Supplies	Asset	Bank Loan	Liability
Machinery	Asset	Taxes Payable	Liability
Equipment	Asset	Retained Earnings	Owners Equity

(B)   (a) increase   (b) decrease   (c) no change

3. The Hula Trio Corp. deposits a check payment from Tunzafun for $315.

(A) Account Name	Type	Account Name	Type
Checking	Asset	Accounts Payable	Liability
Accounts Receivable	Asset	Credit Card	Liability
Office Supplies	Asset	Bank Loan	Liability
Machinery	Asset	Taxes Payable	Liability
Equipment	Asset	Retained Earnings	Owners Equity

(B)   (a) increase   (b) decrease   (c) no change

APPLY

The Income Statement

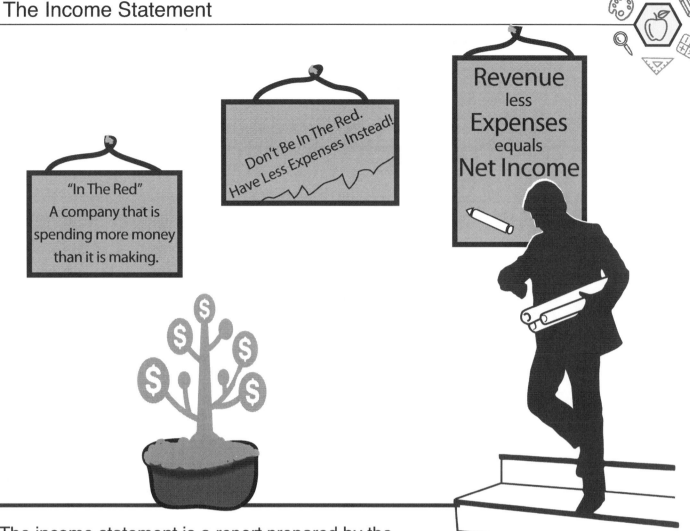

The income statement is a report prepared by the accounting department that shows the net income (profit) for a specific amount of time. The sales are listed as a total in the statement. The money the business spent on expenses is listed in the statement below the sales numbers. The expenses are subtracted from the sales revenue. The answer equals the amount of money the company earned in profit from selling. Revenue, minus expenses, is **net income**.

If the company had revenue (money) from sales that was less than the expenses, the result is known as a **net loss**. A net loss is when the company spends more money than it earned from selling products.

The income statement shows the total profit earned by a business in a specific amount of time. The common business timeframes are a month, quarter, or annual (year) for income statement and balance sheet reports.

Did you know? A net loss may be shown 3 ways.
(1) in parenthesis "( )"
(2) With a negative sign "-" before the number
(3) In red ink

The Drawing Board

Pizza Dough

Review the income statement for Pete Zah's Pizza Place and answer the questions below. The end of year 2020 results are shown, along with a column to compare the end of the year results with 2019.

PETE ZAH'S PIZZA PLACE
Income Statement
Ending December 31, 2019

	2019	2018
Revenue		
Sales	$278,000	$268,000
Less: Coupons and Returns	$ 11,000	$ 1,000
Total Revenue	$267,000	$267,000
Expenses		
Operating Expense	$147,000	$143,000
Production Expense	$ 82,000	$ 78,000
Interest Expense	$ 3,000	$ 3,000
Net Income Before Taxes	$232,000	$224,000
Taxes	$ 12,000	$ 11,000
Total Expenses	$244,000	$235,000
Net Income	$ 23,000	$ 32,000

Did you know ...
Two lines show the final total on a financial statement. (One line shows a sub-total.)

1. Did the sales amount increase or decrease from 2018 - 2019 _____

2. What are the net sales at the end of 2018? _____ and ending 2019? _____

3. If the sales total changed from 2018 to 2019 how is the total revenue number the same?

4. What is a possible reason why production costs increased from 2018 to 2019?

5. How is it possible to have fewer sales, but a higher profit, one year to the next?

6. The company expects sales growth to stay the same. What is an approximate expected sales amount for the end of 2019? _____

THINK

The Gift Of Data

MEAN AVERAGE   MODE   MEDIAN

The accounting department collects information about each payment received and sent, purchases made and returned, and company assets and liabilities. The information is known as data. The gathered data is presented in financial statements to help the company make decisions. Data is a gift to the decision making process since an accurate decision is more likely to be made when understanding past company results.

Wacky Inventors introduced the Oingo Boingo toy last January. There were no other toys like the Oingo Boingo in the marketplace. When a product is unique how can a company set a price for a product? The accounting department and the marketing department will each research and consider different price strategies. The price strategy may change after the product is launched. The company will search to find the price that makes the most profit with the greatest number of customers.

Oingo Boingo — Wacky Industries
12 Month Price History

Price Data:	$49	$45	$40	$34	$34	$29	$29	$34	$34	$39	$45	$38
	JAN	FEB	MAR	APR	MAY	JUN	JUL	AUG	SEP	OCT	NOV	DEC

Imagine you are at your desk on the third floor of Wacky Industries when you receive an e-mail alert. The president of the company has asked for a report summary of the price for the Oingo Boingo.

Using the Oingo Boingo 12 month price history you decide to use math to compute the mean, median, and mode to provide a comparison of the price history. Consider the Oingo Boingo price data above and compute the mean, median, and mode. Be sure to complete a stem and leaf chart to more easily identify the mode.

(1) Mean: _____
    (average)

(2) Median: _____
    (middle)

(3) Mode: _____
    (most common)

(4) Stem and Leaf Chart: | 1st Digit | 2nd Digit |

COMPUTE

The Drawing Board

Let's Dance!

Dance Pals!, a dance school for children, is reviewing three years of business results. Complete the questions below to help the company analyze the results in the five accounts below.

	2018	2019	2020
Rent Paid	$12,000	$14,200	$15,400
Sales	$78,000	$84,000	$90,000
Payroll	$40,000	$45,000	$45,000
Car Loans	$4,000	$22,000	$20,000
Sales Tax Paid	$7,800	$8,400	$9,000

1. Did the company sales from 2018 to 2020 increase, decrease, or stay the same?

     increase   decrease   stay the same

2. What is the amount of the sales change from 2018 to 2020? $_____.

3. What is the amount of the payroll change from 2018 to 2020? $_____.

4. In which year did the company buy a new car with a car loan? $_____.

5. What is the cost of the rent, per month, in 2019? $_____.

6. If the 2 employees at Dance Pals! are paid equally. How much did each employee earn as payroll in 2018? $_____.

7. BONUS:
    What is the sales tax rate in 2020? (a percent of sales) ____%

EXPLORE

Copyright Protected.
www.YMBAgroup.com

Business Ratios

What is a ratio? A ratio is a formula used to compare two numbers to each other. A ratio can help an owner or manager understand the results from the business activities. The results of business activities are recorded in the accounting journals for a business. Business ratios are then computed using accounting information.

How are ratios helpful? Comparing ratios may indicate business results and trends. The trends will help predict future results so the company decisions can be more effective.

What is a "favorable ratio"? A "favorable ratio" is a ratio that has an answer equal to, or better than, company and industry goals.

Only For Corporations That Sell Stock Shares.
(price-earnings ratio)

$$\text{P/E Ratio} = \frac{\text{Stock Market Share Price}}{\text{Earnings Per Share}}$$

A lower answer tells an investor that consumers in the market consider the company to have a low value.

P/E ratio results should be compared with national and industry results to best study the company results.

Does the company have too much debt?

$$\text{D/E Ratio} = \frac{\text{Total Liabilities}}{\text{Total Equity}}$$

The debt to equity ratio shows the amount of debt in a company compared to equity. Equity is the wealth of a company.

A D/E Ratio is considered favorable at less than 1.0. 1.0 says one half of company wealth is needed to pay the company bills.

How much cash is available?

$$\text{Quick Ratio} = \frac{\text{Cash + Accounts Receivable}}{\text{Total Current Liabilities}}$$

A quick ratio result (answer) is favorable when the answer is equal to 1 or higher. An answer of 1 says $2 are available to pay each $1 of debt.

Inventory, equipment, and land needs time to sell, so they are not included as part of the quick cash available.

Is there enough money to pay invoices?

$$\text{Current Ratio} = \frac{\text{Current Assets}}{\text{Current Liabilities}}$$

Cash in the bank account is needed to pay bills. The current ratio only includes current assets (cash or can be cash) and current liabilities (debts paid by company); both are settled in less than one year.

A minimum goal is to have at least double the dollar value in current assets than in current liabilities.

The Drawing Board

Ratio Review

Consider the four ratio examples below. Compare the results with the lesson on the prior page. What do the ratio results reveal about the given company?

1. Fresh Farm Snacks has $23,000 in liabilities and $15,000 in equity. The formula to compute the debt to equity ratio is: $\frac{\$23,000}{\$15,000} = 1.53$
What does the debt to equity ratio answer of 1.53 reveal about the company debt?

2. Maze Florist has $12,000 in current assets and $5,000 in current liabilities. The formula to compute the current ratio is: $\frac{\$12,000}{\$5,000} = 2.4$
What does the ratio answer of 2.4 reveal about how easy it is for a company to pay its bills?

3. Holden Horse Training has $6,000 in cash and $2,000 in accounts receivable. The formula to compute the quick ratio is: $\frac{\$6,000 + \$2,000}{\$5,000} = 1.6$
What does the quick ratio answer of 1.6 reveal about how much cash is available to pay bills?

4. MGL Inc. has a stock price of $7.45 a share and earnings per share of $2. The formula to compute the price earnings ratio is: $\frac{\$7.45}{\$2.00} = 4.23$
What does the ratio answer of 4.23 reveal about the company?

EXPLORE

P/E Ratio - Only For A Company With Stock

The price to buy one share of the company stock on the stock market.

P/E Ratio = $\dfrac{\text{Stock Market Share Price}}{\text{Earnings Per Share}}$

Abbreviated as *EPS* is the dollar amount of earnings (profit) divided by the total number of stock shares owned.

A Lower Number More Likely Pays Higher Dividends

A Dividend Is Paid By A Company To Stock Owners

A price/earnings (P/E) ratio answer is useful to a business investor. If an investor is seeking high returns on their investment finding a company with a lower P/E ratio will be their goal. A P/E ratio does not guarantee the payment of a high dividend, but it can help identify a company that has had earnings and paid shareholders dividends in the past.

Home Builders, Inc.
Established: 1978
Industry: Home Construction
1st Stock Offer: 1981
Current Stock Price: $98.82
Last Years EPS: $14.86
P/E Ratio: 6.30

2019 Construction Industry Average
P/E Ratio: 2.50

IVY Construction, Inc.
Established: 2011
Industry: Home Construction
1st Stock Offer: 2012
Current Stock Price: $38.60
Last Years EPS: $16.08
P/E Ratio: 2.4

Listed in the boxes above are details about Home Builders, Inc. and IVY Construction. Review the information about each company and answer the questions below.

INVESTIGATE

1. Which company is more likely to pay shareholders a higher dividend?

    Home Builders, Inc.   IVY Construction, Inc.

2. Which company has been in business longer?

    Home Builders, Inc.   IVY Construction, Inc.

3. What pieces of information provided did you use to answer question 1?

The Drawing Board

The Board Votes

Castle Construction Company, known as C3, just held a Board of Directors meeting. Decisions were made at the meeting regarding how to spend the company profit. A vote was held and the Board decided to spend some of the company earnings profit on dividends to shareholders, and a portion of the earnings will be invested in business assets.

Use the data below to compute how the Board of Directors at C3 voted to spend the company profit.

Total Number Of Stock Shares Outstanding: 7,934
Total Company Earnings: $ 295,000
Earnings Per Share (EPS): $10.50
Current Stock Market Share Price: $50.00

- The company voted to replace three windows on the building at the total cost of $7,000. The company also voted to replace the roof for $12,000.

- The company voted to purchase 1 enclosed trailer and 1 forklift at a total cost of $12,400 each.

- The company voted to purchase 3 new trucks at a total cost of $18,800 each.

- The company voted to give stockholders a dividend payment equal to 25% of earnings.

1. How much (in dollars) did the Board of Directors at C3 approve to distribute (give) stockholders in dividend payments?

2. What is the total dollar amount approved as either a purchase or a dividend payment?

3. Compute the P/E Ratio. What does the result tell an investor about the company?

COMPUTE

The Ratio Says ...

D/E Ratio

A company with a D/E Ratio of less than 1 has a small amount of debt compared to the value of the business. The lower a D/E Ratio is the higher the overall worth of a company.

For example, Splash Bungee Group has a 0.5 D/E ratio. The D/E ratio of less than one tells business owners and managers that the company needs only a small amount of company money to pay the full balance due on all its debts.

A Favorable Answer Is Less Than 1.0

(Debt to Equity Ratio)

$$\text{D/E Ratio} = \frac{\text{Total Liabilities}}{\text{Total Equity}}$$

Quick Ratio

A company with a Quick Ratio of higher than one is able to pay their bills easily. The more a quick ratio answer is greater than one, the more cash the company has available to pay each invoice due.

A Favorable Answer Is Greater Than 1.0

$$\text{Quick Ratio} = \frac{\text{Cash + Accounts Receivable}}{\text{Total Current Liabilities}}$$

For example, Slurpy Straws has a quick ratio of three. The quick ratio of three shows that the company has $3 available to pay each $1 in debt.

Current Ratio

A company with a Current Ratio of greater than 2 needs less than 50% (half) of the current assets to pay the balance the company owes as current liabilities (due in less than one year).
A company will pay the bills easily with a current ratio greater than 2.0.

For example, the current ratio for Ka-Chu Tissues is 2.5. This informs owners and managers that the company debts are easily paid. The higher the number is above 2.0 shows the more easily a business is able to consider expanding, growing, or buying.

A Favorable Answer Is Greater Than 2.0

$$\text{Current Ratio} = \frac{\text{Current Assets}}{\text{Current Liabilities}}$$

The Drawing Board

Ratio Show & Tell

Listed for each question below are the details needed to compute a ratio. What does the ratio tell the manager or owner about the business operations?

1. Stock Market Share Price: $28.00. Earnings per share: $7.

   The P/E Ratio is _____. This result informs the manager or owner:

2. Total Liabilities: $44,000. Total Equity: $88,000.

   The D/E Ratio is _____. This result informs the manager or owner:

3. Cash Balance: $84,000. Receivables: $4,300. Current Liabilities: $7,700.

   The Quick Ratio is _____. This result informs the manager or owner:

4. Current Assets: $250,000. Current Liabilities: $55,250.

   The Current Ratio is _____. This result informs the manager or owner:

STRATEGIZE

Supply and Demand

Supply — How much should a producer (manufacturer) supply?
As price increases producers want to make more products to sell.

The number of customers to purchase a product depends on the price of the product. For example, imagine if a new computer were offered for $50 ... the inventory would likely sell out the same day! Now, imagine the same new computer was offered at a price of $5,000 ... stock would probably sell slowly. Economics will gather data about how many products are likely to be sold at a given price. The data will be plotted (entered) on a graph. The data points on the graph will be connected with a straight line known as a supply curve.

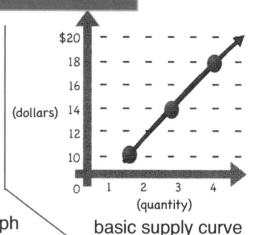
basic supply curve

A product that sells at the higher price (rather than at the lower price for the same product) will make the company more profit. Therefore, as the price for a product increases an increasing number of businesses will want to offer the product to customers.

Supply and Demand curves are reliable when the marketplace is stable (calm).

Demand — How many will customers demand at each price?
As price decreases, demand increases.

The number of products produced by a manufacturer depends on how many customers are willing to buy a product at a price the manufacturer accepts.
For example, imagine if a new flavor juice is demanded by 50,000 people. Many want to purchase the juice, so a manufacturer knows customers want to buy the product. If the new juice demand was only 500 customers, money from juice sales could not pay the production cost.
In this case, a manufacturer will not produce a product to sell.

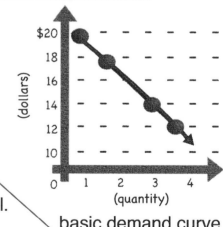
basic demand curve

The data collected will be plotted (entered) on a graph. The data points on the graph will be connected with a straight line to form a demand curve. As a price increases fewer customers will buy the product. Less customers will purchase since the expensive juice is above their budget, or perhaps it is not considered a good price to spend on juice. A producer wants the highest number of customers. Consumers, also known as customers, want a good price and a good product.
As price decreases (goes down) customer demand for the product will increase (go up).

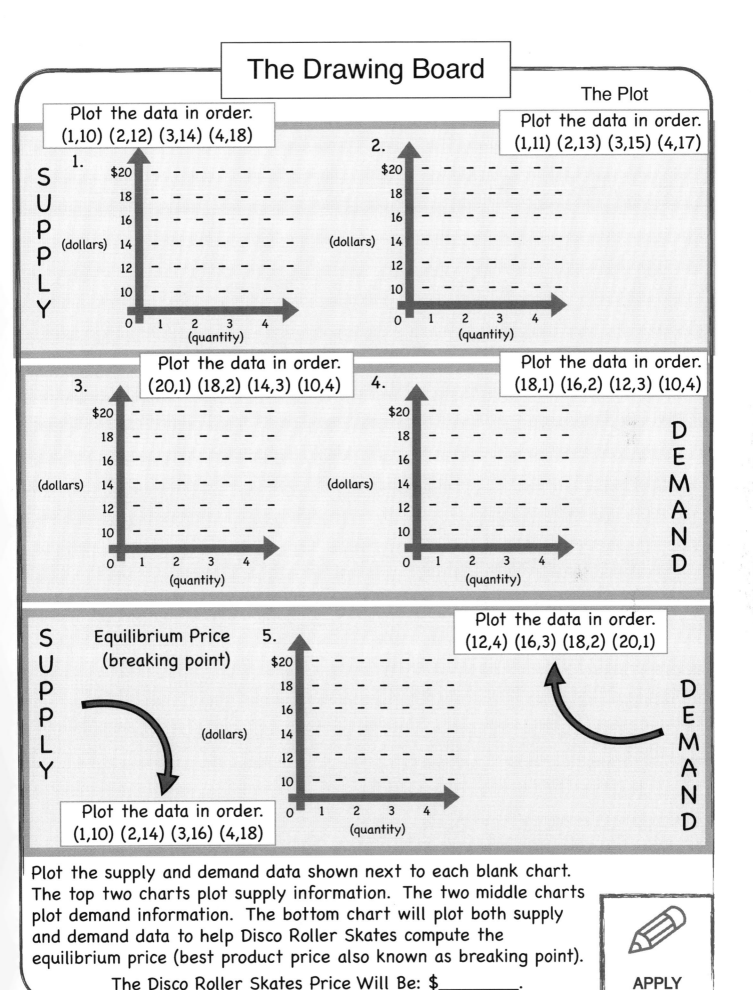

Buy and Sell In A Marketplace

A marketplace is where buyers and sellers meet to buy and sell products. A product may be either a good (sneakers) or a service (haircutting). The price of a product is the amount shoppers believe the item is worth combined with the amount a company will accept.

Marketplace shoppers try to balance what they need and want with what they can afford to spend. To better understand buyers choices, a company will plot supply and demand data. A majority of the data is based on accounting information. The charts will help decision-makers decide on the price for a product or the product quantity. In this way, supply and demand curves, combined with company financial statements, will increase the chance of a business meeting the company goals.

> If enough shoppers do not buy an item there is not enough demand. The price will decrease or the item will no longer be produced for sale.

There are many types of marketplaces in the world. A marketplace is where buyers and sellers meet to buy, sell, and trade goods and services.

EXPLORE

1. How many types of marketplaces where people shop can you list below?

___

2. What is your favorite type of marketplace? Why?

___

The Drawing Board

Supply & Demand

Changes in the marketplace cause changes to what consumers (shoppers) buy. Consumers respond quickly to changes in the marketplace, so a business needs data to react rapidly to market changes as well.

When a company offers a product at a price much lower than the competition demand for the lower-priced product will increase.
When a material needed in the production of a product becomes scarce (difficult to find) the price of the product will increase.
A store will quickly sell all of the shovels when a snowstorm is approaching.

Listed below is a brief description of a decision made by either a producer or consumer. Circle who is the decision-maker (producer or consumer). In the last column circle if the decision was prompted by a change in supply or a change in demand.

Decision	Decision Maker	A Change In
1. The competition just reduced their price 20%. Your company reduces the price 25%.	Producer / Consumer	Supply / Demand
2. Sage granite is becoming more difficult to locate, so manufacturers increase the price.	Producer / Consumer	Supply / Demand
3. Popular history books increase $4, so consumers choose to purchase fewer books.	Producer / Consumer	Supply / Demand
4. A company sells shoelaces for $20 a pair. Consumers do not purchase the product.	Producer / Consumer	Supply / Demand
5. Mango grape ice cream has become so popular a restaurant adds it to the menu.	Producer / Consumer	Supply / Demand

6. Think of a product that you or a family member recently purchased. Write the product name and approximate price below. At what price do you think there would be less demand? At what price will consumers no longer buy the product at all?

_____

_____

_____

INVESTIGATE

Marketplace Sets A Price

An economy that grows quickly will cause prices to increase. But how?

A market that grows too fast will give consumers (buyers) more money to spend. Since more shoppers will be spending money the demand for products will increase. Manufacturers will not have enough time to produce enough, so products become scarce. The short supply of products will cause more demand of the available products. More demand will cause the price of the available products to increase.

With a growing population the economy has to expand, so there are enough items for all the people. Products become scarce when there are not enough products in a market. A government uses interest rates and taxes to help control the growth of an economy. By working to slow down growth manufacturers have time to produce the products consumers demand. Enough products available help keep prices consistent.

A company will sell a product at the highest price possible to have a large number of customers make a purchase.

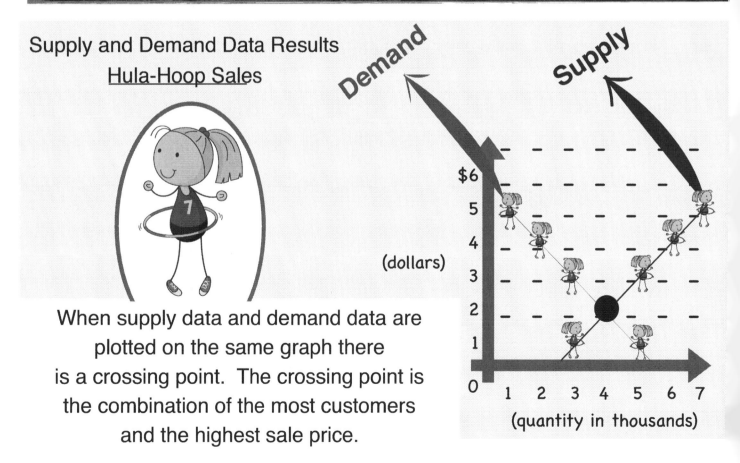

Supply and Demand Data Results
Hula-Hoop Sales

When supply data and demand data are plotted on the same graph there is a crossing point. The crossing point is the combination of the most customers and the highest sale price.

Selling the hula-hoops at $2 each the company can expect 400 to sell.

The Drawing Board

Plot and Predict

A company collects data to help make decisions. Data is often presented on a chart or graph. Data ready to graph is written as two numbers in parenthesis. Example: (5,12)

The first number moves sideways (left to right) along the graph. The second number will move up and down on the graph. Where the two lines intersect (cross) is the breaking point.

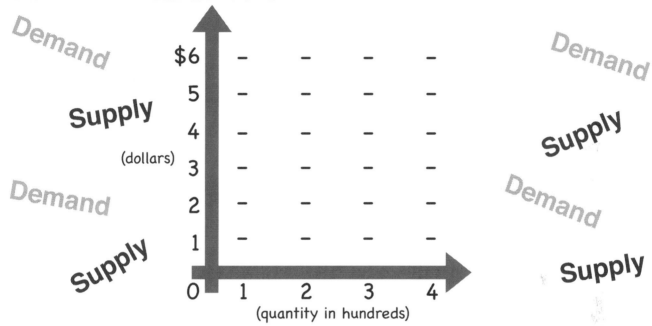

Write the data points in parenthesis. Next, plot all eight points of data above.

SUPPLY DATA

1. 150 sell at a price of $2.00   (_____ , _____)
2. 200 sell at a price of $2.50   (_____ , _____)
3. 300 sell at a price of $3.00   (_____ , _____)
4. 350 sell at a price of $3.50   (_____ , _____)

DEMAND DATA

5. 100 are produced at a sale price of $3.50   (_____ , _____)
6. 200 are produced at a sale price of $3.00   (_____ , _____)
7. 300 are produced at a sale price of $2.50   (_____ , _____)
8. 350 are produced at a sale price of $2.00   (_____ , _____)

APPLY

A Better Budget

A company will prepare a budget each year. The budget will include fixed costs (that do not change), such as the mortgage payment or electric bill. A budget will also include planned expenses such as a new roof or a new computer. The combination of what the company has to spend and what the company wants to spend will create a budget. The budget will let the company know how much the expenses will be each month of the year.

A company budget will also include a best guess at the sales revenue the company will earn in the budget year. A company is able to budget how much they will spend based on the amount they will earn.

The difference between what a company budget expects to earn, less the amount of the company expects to spend, is the profit the company expects to have at the end of the year.

Budget Strategy

A budget is a best guess by the company about the sales and expenses for the upcoming year. A budget is never 100% accurate (correct). For this reason, a budget will be designed with a strategy. A standard company strategy may be to review actual sales and actual expenses each month. The actual budget results would be compared to the expected budget.

For example, a company notices in April that the office supplies expense in March was $1,000, but the company had budgeted to only spend $500 a month on office supplies. A decision may be made not to purchase office supplies in May to balance the budget.
The budget would show $500 in March, April, and May.
The actual spending would show $1000 in March, $500 in April, and $0 in May.

Category	Budget			Actual		
	March	April	May	March	April	May
Office Supplies	$500	$500	$500	$1000	$500	$0
Total	$1,500			$1,500		

The Drawing Board

Asset Accounts

Match the item from the account column to the transaction being described.

Account	Transaction
1. _____ Inventory	A. A purchase is made to stock the toys that sold last month.
2. _____ Accounts Receivable	B. The shirt printer is sent an order for five new employee shirts.
3. _____ Building	C. The company invents a new, unique product design.
4. _____ Office Supplies	D. The company purchases one case of paper.
5. _____ Uniforms	E. A new advertising sign is installed at the building entrance.
6. _____ Patents	F. A customer buys 18 items and the company gives them an invoice with net 10 terms.
7. _____ Interest Earned	G. The company completes the construction of the warehouse expansion.
8. _____ Signage	H. The company checking account receives the monthly interest deposit of $16.

STRATEGIZE

Budget Categories

Chart of Accounts
Cash
Checking
Accounts Receivable
Sales Revenue
Coupons
Office Supplies
Interest Earned
Website Design
Machinery
Equipment
Computers
Education
Maintenance
Repairs
Car Loan
Electric
Telephone
Inventory
Office Cleaning
Water
Printing
Landscaping
Accounts Payable
Mortgage Loan
Interest Payable
Taxes Payable
Marketing
Snow Removal
Inventory
Sales Tax Payable
Truck Repair
Uniforms
and more!

The accounting department organizes all the activities of a company regarding spending or earning. Each time that a product is bought or sold the transaction is recorded into a journal account. The group of accounts is available is known as the *chart of accounts*. The chart of accounts may vary from one company to another, but all will have a cash account, a sales account, and an office supplies account.

A budget with accurate categories will help ensure money is being spent on needed and well-thought-out expenses. Notice that there is not a budget category "miscellaneous" or "other". Budget accounts with too general of a name will easily have items spent and recorded to these accounts. An accurate chart of accounts is most helpful to carefully track spending.

When a company makes a purchase or sells a product, the transaction is recorded by the accounting department. Each transaction will cause a change to two accounts. When one account increases, the other account will decrease.

A budget helps managers and owners plan to spend each month. The planned spending will help make sure that all needed items are purchased, but will also help make sure that each item due is paid on time. By carefully planning and watching company spending a business is more likely to increase its profit.

Did you know ... When a company spends an amount different from the budget it is called a variance. If the budget was $100 but the company spent $80 there was a favorable variance of $20 since the company saved $20.

Did you know ... A good idea is to pay the accounts with a higher interest rate first. The interest rate is what the company is charged for having a loan. Paying the balances with high interest rates first will help save money.

The Drawing Board

Find My Account

Budget Category

TOOLBOX

Inventory	Cash/Checking	Landscaping
Fuel	Office Supplies	Car Loan Payable
Uniforms	Training	Equipment

Review the purchases below. Then select the **two** budget accounts that would change as a result of the purchase transaction. Remember, each purchase will have a change in CASH, ACCOUNTS RECEIVABLE, or a LOAN PAYABLE account to show how the product was paid. A second transaction for each purchase will cause a change in the total dollar balance of an asset or liability account.

(Tool Box accounts may be used more than one time.)

1. A pet store purchases 5 cash registers to use in the store and pays cash.

   Account to increase: _____   Account to decrease: _____

2. A florist purchases a new delivery van and pays with a loan from the bank.

   Account to increase: _____   Account to decrease: _____

3. A baseball team purchases 4 cases of paper and pays with a check.

   Account to increase: _____   Account to decrease: _____

4. A customer purchases 2 dozen gizmos and pays in cash.

   Account to increase: _____   Account to decrease: _____

5. A lawn mowing company purchases 12 gallons of fuel and pays with cash.

   Account to increase: _____   Account to decrease: _____

6. A craft store purchases a forklift and pays with a check.

   Account to increase: _____   Account to decrease: _____

7. The company writes a check for an employee training class.

   Account to increase: _____

   Account to decrease: _____

INVESTIGATE

Macroeconomics - The Big Picture

Macroeconomics researches the overall decisions of all the producers and consumers and the results on the marketplace. Macroeconomics is focused on the overall details of an economy. For example, Macroeconomics does not study a specific company, such as Yellow Corn Company. Macroeconomics does study the overall economic industry of corn or agriculture.

An economy is made up of producers and consumers. Producers decide how goods and services will be produced. Consumers choose which goods and services to purchase.

How does a consumer decide which goods or services will be purchased? A consumer is a shopper who buys goods in the economy. When a product is made well, priced reasonably, and meets the a buyers need, a purchase may be made.	*How does a producer decide how much to make?* The owner of a company will thrive when given the freedom to pursue ideas in business. The owner's goal is to make a profit by selling products. Efficiency means less waste. By having less waste there is more profit for the company.

A market-based economy, such as in the United States, has a goal of growing the economy. The number of people in the United States increases each year. The marketplace needs to grow so that there will be enough jobs, goods, and services, to meet the needs of the growing population. *To make sure the growth is at a stable rate, the government of a country uses taxes and interest rates to help manage an economy.* An economy that is not growing may cause an increase in unemployment or can cause the prices for goods and services to increase.

Did you ever hear or read that jobs were added to the economy? Adding jobs shows an economy has grown, but without knowing how many people were added to the economy during the same timeframe, the number of jobs added alone is not useful data.

Good News!

Population Increase
235,000 People

Economy Added Jobs
241,000 Jobs

The Drawing Board

Puzzle Terms

Complete the crossword puzzle below.
Each answer is an accounting or business term.

Down:
1. The opposite of buy.
3. Another word for a business.
5. The opposite of supply.
7. A statement for a purchase.

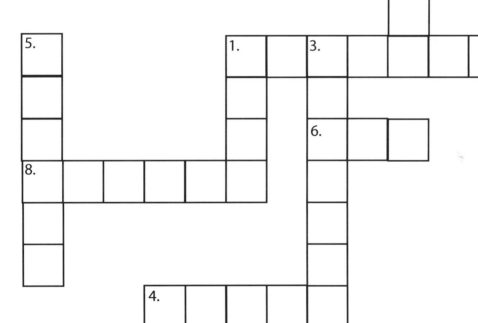

Across:
1. A company hopes a new idea will be a _____.
2. Not a service, but a _____.
4. Another name for a cent, a _____.
6. Abbreviation: Masters of Business Administration.
8. The word used in accounting for 'once a year'.

THINK

Microeconomics - Resources Make Products

Microeconomics studies the business, government, or people that manage the resources that produce a good or service. Microeconomics will also study the marketplace to understand how products get their price.

> Microeconomics tries to predict the availability (or scarcity) of a resource by understanding how production resources are managed and what consumers shopping in the marketplace will pay for the resources.

What is **SCARCITY**? - Scarcity is when there is not enough of a wanted item. When something has low availability and is difficult to purchase, it is scarce.

What is **PRODUCTION**? - The process of making a product from resources.

What are **RESOURCES**?
The 4 M's of resources
Manpower, Money, Machines, Materials
The resources available or needed when producing (making) a good or service.

What is **EFFICIENCY**?
Using resources with the least amount of production waste.

What is **PRODUCTION WASTE**?
When resources are not used efficiently. Waste can be a waste of time, a waste of money, or a waste of materials.

Did you hear about the problem with the new t-shirt sewing machine?

You bet! What a waste of time that it has to stop to cool every 45 minutes.

Any chance you saw the scrap material the new t-shirt sewing machine leaves?

Very concerning, that wasted resource is like seeing money tossed on the floor.

> **THE PRODUCTION GOAL**
> **USE RESOURCES EFFECTIVELY.**
> **EVERY BARREL HAS A BOTTOM.**

The Drawing Board

Meet The Teacher

Welcome to our class. Today you are joining a corporate training seminar about production and efficiency. Select the word or term from the toolbox to match the microeconomics topic being discussed.

The instructor says, "That brings us to the part of the day where each class member will share one production concern in their department. As a group you will brainstorm to develop with suggestions. Remember, brainstorming is when a series of ideas are discussed, but we are not yet selecting a solution.

1. I am in the marketing department. When we need only a few flyers we can print them ourselves. But, our printer ink does not work well until about the 5th copy. Each time a new print job is run we have four pages we throw in the trash. The economic term being described here is: _____

2. I am in the shipping department. I am concerned about our _____. When a rush order needs to be shipped we are slowed down by making boxes. This causes a rush order to be delayed until a box is ready so it can ship.

3. I am in the purchasing department. The color fabric chosen for the Daisy Flower toy line is very popular. It is in such high demand the price keeps going up - and I still can not find enough to buy. The fabric chosen by the design team is so hard to locate; it is showing signs of _____. Production needs more of this _____ to continue the production of the toy.

4. I am in the management office. We noticed that when the _____ of of the Rumble Bumble Truck was lowered that the demand for the truck got very high. Consumers bought them faster than _____ could make them!

Terms

TOOLBOX

Production Waste   Resource   Production
Scarcity   Price   Efficiency

APPLY

Case Study - Green Grass Lawn Mowing

Imagine you are a consultant. Today you have an appointment with your client. The client is the owner of the Green Grass Lawn Mowing Company.

You ask: Good afternoon, how may I help you today?

(1) Client says: My lawnmower needs to be replaced. Should I get a top of the line lawnmower, or just a basic lawnmower to finish the lawn season?

You ask: When does your busy season start again?

Client says: In about six months, so I think I will buy a basic mower for now with cash. Then I will use a loan to buy the better lawn mower in 6 months.

You ask: If you save money for six months can you buy the mower in cash?

(3) Client says: I have the cash now but do not want to spend the money. The cost of the lawn mower in six months will leave my bank account with only $100.

You ask: Did you decide on the company storage unit? Will you combine the two rental units into one rental unit to save money?

(5) Client says: The units both feel so organized to me. The rent is $120 a month for each unit, so a bit high, but the space is nice.

You ask: Perhaps now that the slow season has started you will have the time. Do you have any plans for the slow season? Have you found a job?

(7) Client says: I was offered two jobs. The first was as a manager for the holidays at my favorite store. The second was as a sports coach. I chose the sports coach.

You ask: Perhaps if you chose the retail manager job you could buy the top of the line lawn mower for cash?

(9) Client says: Now that is a good idea! I will choose the retail store manager job for the holidays.

You say: Glad I could help.

Client says: Accountants sure know how to make decisions with the business numbers!

Copyright Protected.

The Drawing Board

Case Analysis

After reading the case study on the previous page about the business operations at Green Grass Lawn Mowing Company consider the questions below. Match the number in the case study to the odd question number's below.

1. What did the company choose to do? _____

2. What would you choose to do?

3. What did the company choose to do? _____

4. What would you choose to do?

5. What did the company choose to do? _____

6. What would you choose to do?

7. What did the company choose to do? _____

8. What would you choose to do?

9. What did the company choose to do? _____

10. What would you choose to do?

STRATEGIZE

This page intentionally left blank.

Y.M.B.A. Accounting Review

Congratulations on completing the Y.M.B.A. Accounting learning workbook. Consider the questions below to demonstrate all you have learned. Write your answers in the spaces provided on the answer page.

1. _____ keeps the record of the revenue and expenses of a company.

    (A) Marketing   (B) Accounting   (C) Finance   (D) Laws

2. The most popular and wanted asset in a business is _____.

    (A) Cash   (B) Cars   (C) Computers   (D) Costs

3. LIFO stands for Last In, ____ Out.

    (A) Fast   (B) Final   (C) First   (D) Four

4. FIFO is a method for determining the value of _____.

    (A) A Business   (B) Interest   (C) Inventory   (D) Bank Accounts

5. A loan that will take 20 years to pay to zero dollars is a _____ term liability.

    (A) Long   (B) Short   (C) Tall   (D) Wide

6. The company records the money owed from customers in accounts _____.

    (A) Receivable   (B) Expected   (C) Payable   (D) Past Due

7. A current asset is cash or can become cash in _____ or less.

    (A) 1 day   (B) 1 quarter   (C) 1 year   (D) 1 month

8. Revenue less expenses is the company _____.

    (A) Tax Rate   (B) Debt   (C) Liabilities   (D) Profit

9. Paying back a loan a small portion each month is an _____ loan.

    (A) Important   (B) Installment   (C) Instant   (D) Impact

Copyright Protected.   www.YMBAgroup.com

10. When a company has more expenses than sales it is a net _____.
    (A) Loan   (B) Loss   (C) Lose   (D) Lost

11. A public company sells stock and pays shareholders _____.
    (A) Dollars   (B) Deposits   (C) Dividends   (D) Debts

12. The abbreviation EPS stands for _____ Per Share.
    (A) Earnings   (B) Evaluations (C) Events   (D) Entry

13. As _____ increases the demand for a product decreases.
    (A) People   (B) Price   (C) Places   (D) Profits

14. Buyers and sellers come together in a _____ to buy and sell.
    (A) Marketplace (B) Group   (C) Gathering   (D) Majority

15. When a customer buys a product and will pay later they receive a/an _____.
    (A) Balance Sheet (B) Invoice (C) Deposit Slip (D) Picture

16. _____ is when there is not enough of a resource to meet demand.
    (A) Liabilities (B) Scarcity   (C) Debt   (D) Expenses

17. To use _____ with the least amount of waste is known as efficiency.
    (A) Trucks   (B) Cash   (C) Resources   (D) Revenue

18. Revenue less expenses equals net income is shown on the _____ statement.
    (A) Income   (B) Interest   (C) Internet   (D) Invention

19. Cash, inventory, office supplies and computers are all _____ assets.
    (A) Tangible   (B) Terrific   (C) Touch   (D) Trumpet

20. A company is "In The Red" when it is _____ more than it is earning.
    (A) Sales   (B) Saving   (C) Stocking   (D) Spending

21. Starting a business involves a high amount of _____.
    (A) Return (B) Risk (C) Reward (D) Range

22. The _____ of a company may be found on the balance sheet.
    (A) Prices (B) Sales (C) Products (D) Assets

23. An asset you can not touch is an _____ asset.
    (A) Interesting (B) Invoice (C) Intangible (D) Interest Rate

24. The month of _____ is in the second quarter of the fiscal year.
    (A) March (B) April (C) July (D) October

25. The assets of a company that are available for sale to customers are _____.
    (A) Inventory (B) Sales (C) Profits (D) Coupons

26. The debt to equity ratio with liabilities of $24,000 and equity of $12,000 is _____.
    (A) 1.2 (B) 2.0 (C) 2.2 (D) 20

27. _____ select which products to buy in the marketplace.
    (A) Consumers (B) Sellers (C) Investors (D) Manufacturers

28. If customers want an increasing amount of a product the _____ is growing.
    (A) Resource (B) Supply (C) Cost (D) Demand

29. The item that belongs in the office supplies account category is _____.
    (A) Landscaping (B) Copy Paper (C) Roof Repair (D) Taxes Payable

30. A company buys 5 uniforms at $20 each. The uniform account increases _____.
    (A) $25 (B) $100 (C) $250 (D) $520

31. A long-term liability account would be _____.

   (A) Mortgage   (B) Water   (C) Fuel   (D) Marketing

32. The term Net 15 on an invoice indicates the customer has _____ days to pay.

   (A) 5   (B) 10   (C) 15   (D) 20

33. The balance sheet shows the total _____, liabilities, and owners equity.

   (A) Revenues   (B) Expenses   (C) Sales   (D) Assets

34. The four P's of marketing are product, place, promotion and _____.

   (A) Pictures   (B) People   (C) Price   (D) Presentations

35. The four M's of resources are manpower, money, machines and _____.

   (A) Materials   (B) Motion   (C) Mission   (D) Monthly

36. A credit card with a balance due is a business _____.

   (A) Equity   (B) Asset   (C) Revenue   (D) Liability

37. When a company makes a purchase but does not pay, _____ increases.

   (A) Supplies   (B) Cash   (C) Loans Payable   (D) Accounts Payable

38. Find the median number in the data group: 12, 14, 15, 16, 18

   (A) 15   (B) 16   (C) 18   (D) not shown

39. A company buys five radio commercials. The expense is recorded in the account:

   (A) Marketing   (B) Uniforms   (C) Office Supplies   (D) Landscaping

40. Where the supply and demand data points cross is the _____ point.

   (A) Comparison   (B) Balance   (C) Breaking   (D) Cross

Y.M.B.A. Accounting Review Student Test Sheet

Consider the questions on the previous four pages.
Write your answers in the spaces provided below.

1. _____   11. _____   21. _____   31. _____

2. _____   12. _____   22. _____   32. _____

3. _____   13. _____   23. _____   33. _____

4. _____   14. _____   24. _____   34. _____

5. _____   15. _____   25. _____   35. _____

6. _____   16. _____   26. _____   36. _____

7. _____   17. _____   27. _____   37. _____

8. _____   18. _____   28. _____   38. _____

9. _____   19. _____   29. _____   39. _____

10. _____   20. _____   30. _____   40. _____

This page intentionally left blank.

Certificate of Completion

Presented To

_____

Upon Successful Completion

of the

Youth Master of Business Administration

ACCOUNTING

_____
Presented By

_____
Date

© www.YMBAgroup.com

Y.M.B.A. Accounting Drawing Board Answer Key

Page 9: (1) 21 (2) $12,325 (3) $862.75 (4) $12,325-$3,045=$9,280 (5) $3,625

Page 11: (1) b (2) a (3) a (4) b (5) b (6) b (7) a (8) a (9) a (10) b

Page 13: (1) 16 x $6=$96 (2) 52 x $12 =$624 (3) 214 x $2.50=$535 (4) 25 x $50=$1,250

Page 14: (1) $1.00 x 44=$44 (2) $1.24 x 20= $24.80 (3) $44 + $24.80=$68.80

Page 15:

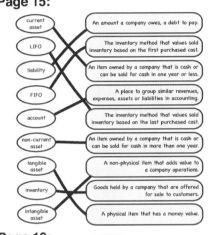

Page 19:

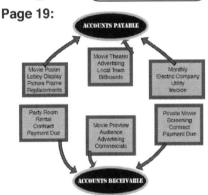

Page 21: (1) $9,000 (2) $33,900 (3) $21,600 (4) $12,400

Page 23: (1) $2,000 (2) $200 (3) $6,000 (4) $42,000 (5) $30,600 (6) $75,000 (7) $21,000 (8) $130,000 (9) $182,000 (10) $2,800 (11) $4,000 (12) $60,800 (13) $74,800

Page 25: (1) b (2) a (3) b (4) a (5) a (6) a (7) January (8) April, May, June

Page 27: (1) varies, one answer circled (2) varies, four answers circled (3) varies, answers should logically be part of the overall expense category.

Page 28: answers will vary, blank spaces should have a reply to match the clue under the line.

Page 29: (1) answer should include that inventory is needed for the new customers.

(2) by knowing how many satisfy one zip code the company can use math to solve how many are needed for three more. (3) the current 4 employees multiplied by 3 more zip codes equals 12 new employees.

Page 31: (1) (a) machinery and bank loan (b) no change (2) (a) checking and credit card (b) decrease (3) (a) checking and accounts receivable (b) increase

Page 33: (1) increase (2) both years are $267,000 (3) more coupons and returns (4) higher prices or ordered more (5) more expenses or more coupons given (6) $288,000

Page 34: (1) $37.50 (add prices from the 12 months and divide by 12) (2) 34 and 38 are the two middle numbers, so they are averaged to get a median 36. (3) mode is the most common, 34 (4)

1st	2nd
2	9,9,9
3	4,4,4,4,8
4	0,5,5,9

Page 35: (1) increase (2) $90,000 - $78,000 = $12,000 (3) $45,000 - $40,000 = $5,000 (4) 2013 (5) $14,200 divided by 12 months = $1,183.33 (6) $40,000 divided by 2 = $20,000 (7) $90,000 divided by $9,000 = .10, as a percent 10% sales tax.

Page 37: (1) the company has little debt. (2) there is cash easily available to pay all bills. (3) the company may have difficulty paying bills since less than 2. (4) the company may pay dividends, but not a low p/e ratio so not likely high dividends.

Page 38: (1) home builders (2) ivy construction (3) low p/e ratio shows dividends, if paid, a low dollar amount.

Page 39: (1) $295,000 x .25 = $73,750 (2) $21,000+$12,000+ $24,800+$56,400+$73,750= $187,950 (3) $50 divided by $10.50=high p/e dividends high

Page 41: (1) $28/$7=$4, high p/e so high dividends if paid. (2) $44,000/$88,000=.5, low d/e so the company can easily pay bills (3) ($84,000+$4,300)/$7,700=11.48 very high quick ratio, bills easily paid. (4) $250,000/$55,250=4.52, above 2 so company needs less than half of assets to pay bills.

Page 43: (1) $16 (breaking point)

Page 44: (1) varies, all places where people buy or sell (2) varies

Page 45: (1) producer/demand (2) producer/supply (3) consumer/ demand (4) consumer/demand (5) producer/demand (6) varies

Page 47: (1) (1.5,2) (2) (2,2.5) (3) (3,3) (4) (3.5,3.5) (5) (1,3.5) (6) (2,3) (7) (3,2.5) (8) (3.5,2)

Page 49: (1) A (2) F (3) G (4) D (5) B (6) C (7) H (8) E

Page 51: (1) office supplies/cash (2) car loan/loan payable (3) office supplies/checking (4) inventory/cash (5) fuel/cash (6) equipment/checking (7) training/checking

Page 53: Down (1) sell (3) company (5) demand (7) invoice **Across** (1) success (2) good (4) penny (6) MBA (8) annual

Page 55: (1) production waste (2) efficiency (3) scarcity/resource (4) price/production.

Page 57: 1,3,5,7,9 see p. 57, even numbers answers vary.

Y.M.B.A. Accounting Review Answer Key

1. B
2. A
3. C
4. C
5. A
6. A
7. C
8. D
9. B
10. B

11. C
12. A
13. B
14. A
15. B
16. B
17. C
18. A
19. A
20. D

21. B
22. D
23. C
24. B
25. A
26. B
27. A
28. D
29. B
30. B

31. A
32. C
33. D
34. C
35. A
36. D
37. D
38. A
39. A
40. C

Y.M.B.A. Single Topic Learning Workbooks

Lesson Pages, Worksheets, A Quiz and A Certificate

Learn Life Skills & Business with Y.M.B.A.

Benefit from 100 top tips and tricks that will enhance the effectiveness and enjoyment of your internet-based virtual classroom presented by virtual teacher, recruiter and trainer, L.J. Keller. A must-have book for anyone considering, or currently teaching, English virtually as a second language! Benefit from ideas, techniques and examples for English lanugage learners. These easy to implement concepts can enhance your classroom and effectively increase your students comprehension. Students also enjoy learning in this active learner classroom environment. Ideas are presented with clarity using examples that can provide you with a competitive advantage in the virtual classroom. Enjoy this all-in-one solution to help you launch and sustain amazing student results.
Are you ready to be an amazing virtual teacher?

Do you know someone who would like to work from home? Virtual teaching is a wonderful option! Work from home. Flexible schedules. Amazing students!

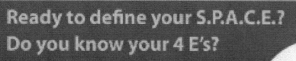

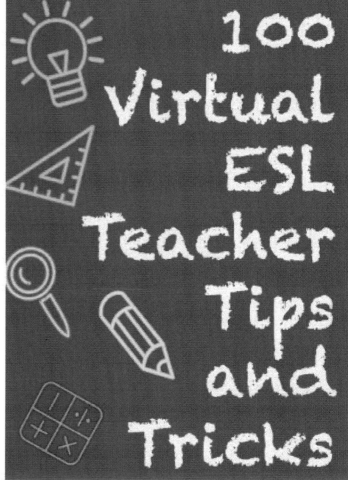

This one book can help you quickly achieve a successful virtual classroom.

100 Tips are ready to assist!

Recruiting for virtual teachers with a four year college degree, any major at:
www.YMBAgroup.com

SPLASH: A waterpark mystery

The champion is part of a secret plan! Solve the mystery as you meet Battle, twins Rachel and Reese, Zack and Morgan as they travel the United States with their parents. In this first book in the series the family begins a road trip adventure. The first *family fun stop* finds a mystery the family works together to solve. Join the family as they race to tell the judges. What was the secret plan? How will the kids find the judges to stop the results in time? What is discovered?
Grades 2-4/Ages 6-8/Early Chapter Book

Look Inside!

Skill Builder practice and a Book Quiz Included

Engaging Reading Books plus Skill Builders & a Book Quiz An easy way to demonstrate learning accomplishments.

Chapter Books That Are Fun To Read and Include A Quiz To Demonstrate Completion

57 Days Miriam Short Sails With William Penn

Join Miriam, Adam and Anne Mary, on their journey from England to America with William Penn to see the land he was granted in the New World by the King of England. Exciting history based on actual people and events. Experience the triumphs, struggles, loss and dreams while traveling across the Atlantic Ocean to a new home. Discover the path so many experienced as they left their home for America. Details vividly paint a picture of the conditions on the ship and the difficult days along the way. What challenges did they endure?
What were the fears and hopes of the young adults?
An exciting historical adventure of the journey to America. Join Miriam on her voyage with her family and William Penn.
GRADES 6-10/AGES 11-15/ FACTION CHAPTER BOOK

Available on AMAZON.com and retail sites such as BarnesandNoble.com

Printed by Amazon Italia Logistica S.r.l.
Torrazza Piemonte (TO), Italy